The Millionaire Beach Club

David Galindo Rivera

DISCLAIMER

For personal safety reasons, the location of the beach is not disclosed. This occurred over six years ago.

DEDICATION

This manuscript is dedicated to my Godmother, Martha.

She has always been here for me.

Thank you for the amazing "free" face masks you provided for

me and all others during this horrible Covid-19 pandemic.

She served El Paso, Texas for over 20 years as a former

emergency room long-term charge nurse.

You are an amazing example for all of humanity.

I love you.

ACKNOWLEDGEMENTS

First, thank you my Lord and Savior, Jesus Christ. You always provide the words to my manuscripts. The Holy Spirit is alive and well.

Thank you again, Isoya, for finding the time between your college work to create the amazing artwork!

My best friend, Belinda is an amazing proofreader. Thank you for your unconditional love.

Accomplished writer, Ernesto Patino, helped me again. Thank you.

PROLOGUE

Traveling is amazing. It is a way to grow and educate yourself.

I have been fortunate enough to experience seven different

countries.

Due to circumstances, you will sometimes have to endure the

worst of things. This is a moment in time to show an

unconscionable nature of humanity.

Will you believe this story?

DAY ONE

It has been raining intensely for the past two days. As

backpackers, we always walked to explore. Getting sick is out of

the question. This would ruin our seven-day vacation.

Someone mentioned a beach with supposedly minimal rain.

With nothing to lose, we arrived within 45 minutes. The taxi

driver seemed surprised to be taking us here.

It was sprinkling rain with a dark overcast tone. Some locals

noticed us as they sat on the street curb.

We soon walked upon a beautiful hotel by the *sea*. The hotel

owners were guarded but still welcomed us.

Our spacious room had a big window.

"Look how sunny it is now!" my partner shouted.

 We immediately left to go into the water.

Without hesitation, people tried to sell us anything from fruit to

cigars. A destitute man became persistent and would not leave

us alone.

"Be careful here!" warned another observing man.

I will always remember the movie scene when Leonardo

DiCaprio and his friends arrived at "The Beach." This was

comparable.

We were easy to spot: She is tall and pretty; carrying an umbrella. I am muscular with long black hair.

The water was so warm and clear. You could even see the fish swimming near you. It was an amazing and wonderful feeling.

"We will take four more days of this!" she contented. I also agreed.

After spending two hours in the water, we headed back to the hotel.

On the main street, street vendors sold necklaces, bracelets and other collectible items.

One of them grabbed my partner aggressively! He would not "take no" for an answer. This is considered a crime in the United States. We bought a couple of his shirts after agreeing to stay away from his business.

The hotel was clean. The beds were comfortable, but there was a mysterious woman sobbing through the night...

DAY TWO

We got up early to go into the water. It was already sunny.

Some people were walking around with metal detectors; and

young baseball players were pitching to each other.

After breakfast, we explored the beach. She used the umbrella

to repel the sun.

We had just walked a mile when someone instantly shouted,

"Haha, look at those American pussies!"

 Five men sat on their lounge chairs. They had the same swim

trunks with similar tattoos.

My travel partner looked at me.

"Keep walking Jnnier, keep walking!"

"Hehe, that's what we thought."

"American pussies!"

"Hey, let's find a coffee house with Wi-Fi access," I asked

quietly.

To our horror, the internet identified the tattoos. They

were @us&ian mafia symbols.

Thankfully, there were a lot of people on this beach. We

decided to keep exploring but with, *our eyes wide open*. It was

already a busy Thursday.

"Oh boy, check out these shady characters…"

More and more individuals engaged in what appeared to be criminal enterprise.

Good and bad people will always exist but, you cannot judge

someone just because they look scary.

At this point, we wanted to find activities to keep us occupied.

Suddenly, an English-speaking man introduced himself. He

was interested in showing us around.

I will never forget the predatory look on his face.

I shook my head, no.

You should always follow your first instinct. It is usually spot on.

Before arriving back at the hotel, we noticed an interesting

sign.

It said in Spanish to "Report child trafficking."

Later in the evening, we chose an Italian restaurant.

Then at that moment: she noticed something from the kitchen.

"Oh my God, it's Junior from the Sopranos!"

She ran into the kitchen to take pictures of the head cook as I

watched in horror.

"Are you trying to get us killed? Get back over here!"

The head cook soon came out. Then, he took off his hat to glare

at us.

"Why did you do that?"

"I can't believe it's Junior from the Sopranos. He is the head cook here!" she explained.

"Please, don't do that again! It's not Junior. He is just someone who looks like him."

The cook decided to let it go after studying my travel partner. Surprisingly, the food was excellent.

Afterwards, the main street had many people conducting illegal business as usual. There were a lot of prostitutes walking around trying to entice men. It appears non-violent crime is commonplace. Staying quiet is the best defense here. We decided "not" to investigate the crying woman.

DAY THREE

The baseball players were practicing again, but there were no

metal detectors.

Today, the water had many animals such as starfish.

A grouper fish kept interacting with me. It was softly pinching

my leg. I was amazed to be playing with an animal.

I believe: It possessed the spirit of my late grandma, Anna.

She would always playfully pinch my legs with her toes.

Soon thereafter, I see my partner talking to a very tall man. He

was displaying a starfish in the middle of his giant hand.

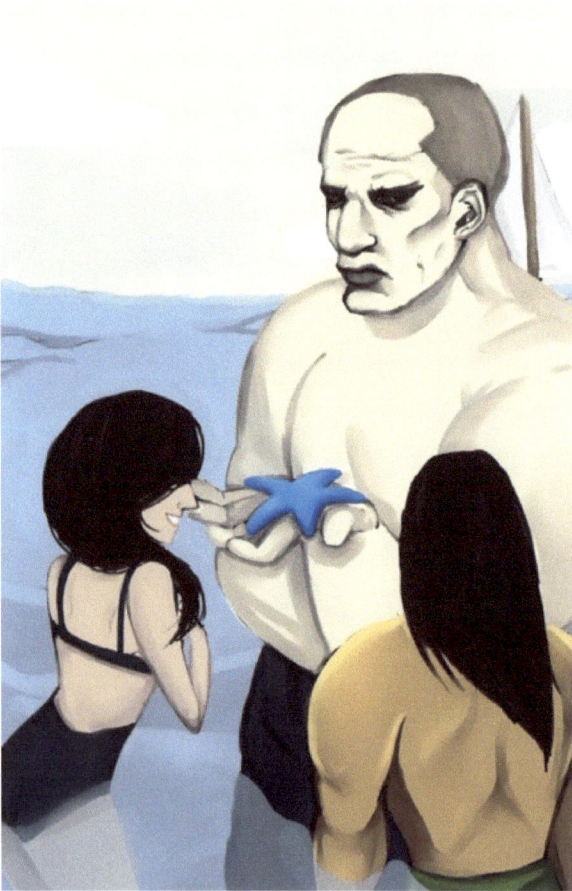

"I work for Mussolini when I was young."

His eyes were an ice-cold blue as he stared at me after speaking in broken English.

I could not fathom the number of people this man already had killed and tortured.

He was the most physically fit 90-something year old.

He mentioned swimming here 3 times a week with a plethora of push-ups, sit-ups and jump squats.

We decided to explore the beach again after breakfast at the hotel.

As usual, there were a lot of shady looking people conducting business.

Why is this beach unknown? There had to be a reason…

"Hey come in here. We have the best seafood!" shouted an English speaking scouter.

"Do you serve paella?" my partner asked.

"Indeed, we do!"

Several men lounged in front of the open-air restaurant.

The restaurant employees studied us as we sat.

A 12-year-old boy was sitting by himself. He looked kind of

guarded but aware of something about to happen.

Then, one of the employees walked to the lounging area to

bring in six European men.

My partner recognized the language they spoke.

"Oh, they are @er%an."

She offered to take a group picture with one of their phones.

The restaurant employees became more relaxed after seeing

this. The men surrounded the boy like a pack of wolves.

Fifteen minutes later, we see another man escorted into the

restaurant.

He looked like a typical expat in his 50's.

Out of nowhere, a five-year-old boy runs out with balloons.

The man grabbed the child and put him on his lap.

He was petting the boy's legs and butt.

I will never forget his ugly demonic look.

The child was acting like it was his birthday because he

had been deceived.

He had no idea what was about to happen.

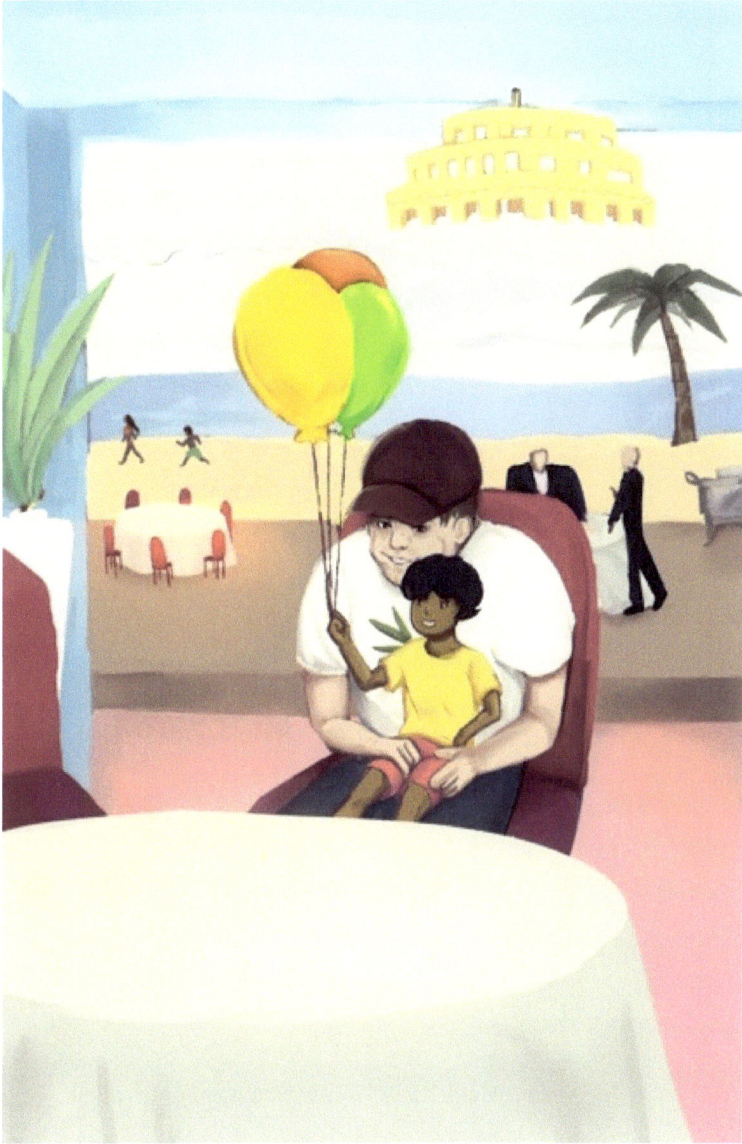

I looked at my travel partner and said, "Let's get the hell out of here!"

I almost vomited from disgust.

This was the first time I had ever witnessed anything like this.

We were eating at a restaurant "front" for pedophiles!

The child traffickers noticed us leaving abruptly.

As we left, something told me to go to a well-known bank.

Believe it or not, this foreign country had it.

I reported a lost or stolen debit card.

I had them call an American branch notifying our whereabouts.

Now, the bank had a record of the phone call.

We then went back to the hotel. I suggested transferring into another room with no windows.

She asked, "Why?"

"Just for safety," I recommended.

"Ok..." she agreed.

"It's better to be safe than sorry. Does this happen in all countries? This is horrific!" I protested.

There is nothing eviler than taking advantage of children. They are all innocent.

We talked about this but decided to accept it.

Tourists are subject to whatever is normal in foreign countries.

Being arrested for disturbing "their sense of peace," was out of

the question.

Dinner was served at a "boat" restaurant.

It was a beautiful early evening, but the restaurant owner was

curious of us. He was an expat, who talked about the

importance of keeping secrets.

He ended the conversation with a smile; and then, playfully

smacked my shoulder. Was this a veiled threat or not? I let it

go though so we could eat dinner in peace.

Back at the hotel, the woman was still weeping.

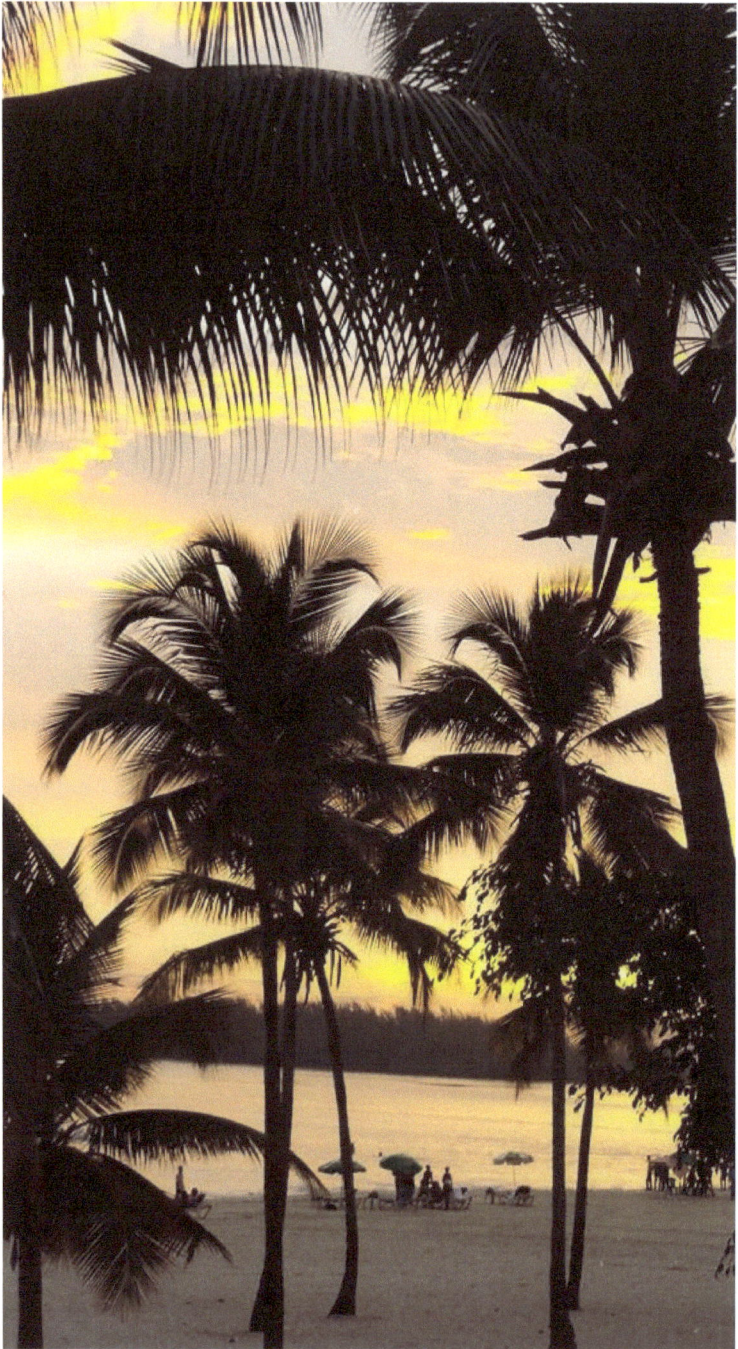

DAY FOUR

We stayed one more day because she loved the water.

The hotel employees were unusually quiet during breakfast.

It was a very weird morning.

On the beach, everything you could imagine was on display.

It was a very festive Saturday.

For lunch, we ate red snapper with coconut milk and oil.

My partner still had not processed the peril of our situation.

I thought about this as I ate.

Is this the reason she has always been successful traveling?

Are violent predators only receptive to the distressed?

As I was thinking and eating, a handsome young man appeared.

He continued to walk around our table.

This aggravated me; so, I took off my sunglasses to stare at him.

He then raised his left arm; to display a tattoo on the left side of

his body.

It was the grim reaper holding onto a severed head!

Finally, before leaving: He took off his sunglasses to show me his "dead shark eyes."

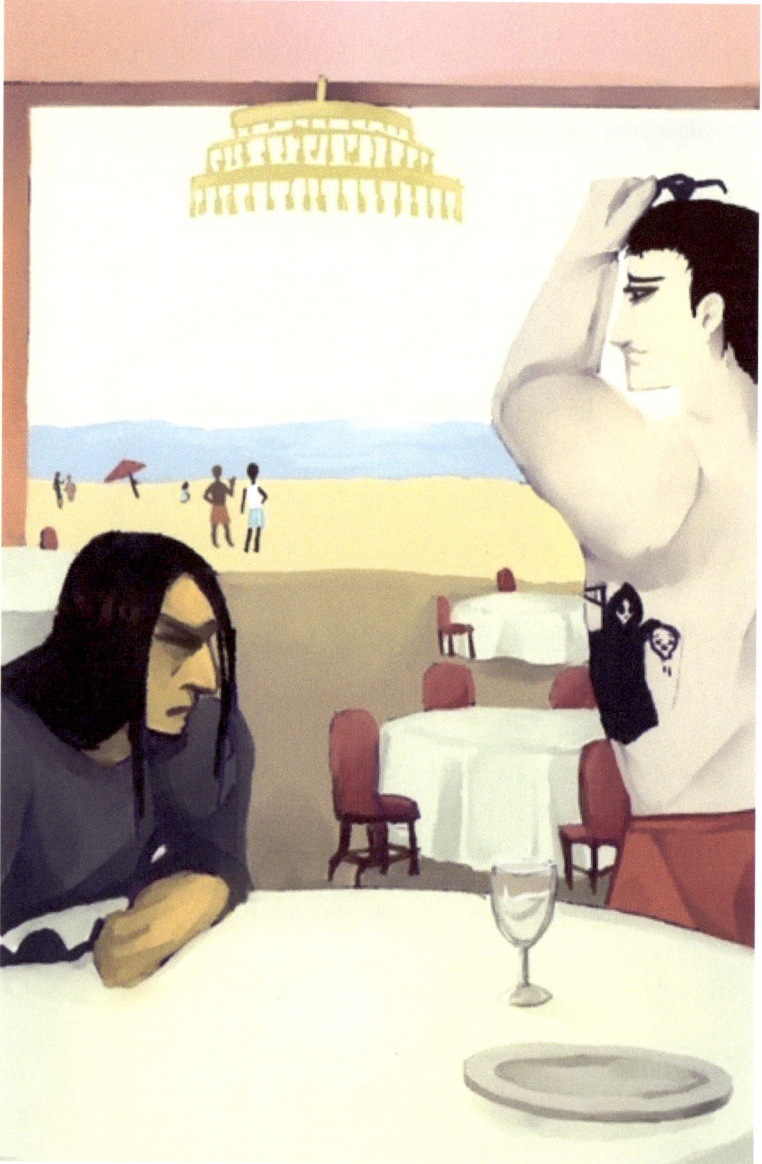

"Maybe we should leave this beach now," I warned.

"I don't think anything will happen to us with all these people being here," she countered.

"Then, let's go back to the hotel!" I insisted.

It was the sunniest and most beautiful day of our vacation.

Because of this: we decided to go into the water for a final time.

There were hundreds of people on the beach.

As we entered the ocean water, more and more people started entering the water too.

"Hey, they are walking toward us," she observed.

"Yeah, I think we should leave," I recommended.

"It looks like they want to attack us," she trembled.

"Ok, keep close to me!"

We walked through a gauntlet of people as they were mumbling obscenities and looking horribly at us.

Indeed, being muscular is a deterrent to violence.

Maybe, most tourists participate in illegal activities offered at

this beach. We never did. As a result, they probably thought

we were investigating something.

It's not fun being singled out by the consensus.

"Do you think we are in danger?" she asked.

"I think we are still ok but, we should return to a familiar

restaurant."

At the Italian restaurant, the owner introduced himself to us.

It turned out that he had family in our home state.

That night, we prepared for our departure.

I was paranoid and could not sleep.

Interestingly, the woman was not heard again...

DAY FIVE

My partner woke up at sunrise and wanted to go for a walk.

She still refused to buy into the perilousness of our situation.

As we walked, motorcycle taxis stopped to make frantic phone calls. They were reporting our whereabouts to someone. This really spooked us out.

We went to the Italian restaurant for breakfast because it had Wi-Fi access.

Here, it would be unlikely to be taken by force.

I finally researched danger warnings around neighboring towns.

There had been many reports of violence, kidnapping and death within the past 6 months.

Then, I showed her this...

"Let's get the hell out of here, now!" she demanded.

It took the internet to realize the danger.

At the hotel, we begged the owners to do the right thing.

She lied by saying, "Authorities of power have been contacted in the United States."

We compensated the owners after they called a friend to transport us to the airport.

The ride out of the beach town was eerie.

People were watching us leave. One motorcycle followed us but finally changed direction.

At the airport, there was some trouble with immigration, but we managed to make it through.

We had several hours before boarding.

It was imperative to stay quiet.

During this time, many thoughts crossed my mind.

Suddenly, I had an epiphany…

We just spent five days at "The Millionaire beach club!"

Wealthy and rich people traveled there to enjoy expensive taboos without worry. It was not quite Sodom and Gomorrah because the Mafia kept control of everything.

Is this in the background at major cities like New York and Chicago?

Clearly, pedophilia is beyond what is acceptable today. I hope it never gets to this point in America.

Then, I remembered meeting my friend's family maid during grade school.

"Mom why don't we have maids?"

I will never forget, her grave stare.

"Because you and your brother were molested by them!"

I never recalled the molestation.

I have always struggled trusting people. I am a sex and alcohol addict. I have been arrested twice already.

Maybe, this is the reason why.

I could not imagine this being a regular part of my childhood.

I could not have survived such a life.

It is so horrific and evil to be a commodity here!

People turned the other cheek.

Remember, crime was commonplace at this beach.

Humanity is in serious trouble when this starts occurring everywhere without any outrage.

"Hey, it's time to board!" my partner yelled.

"Ok let's go." I said relieved.

As our plane took off, I looked at my her and said, "You know, we are lucky to be alive."

"We just survived, The Millionaire Beach Club!"

I hugged her as she cried.

She then said, "GOD BLESS AMERICA!"

EPILOGUE

How many millionaire beach clubs already exist?

Is America, the largest millionaire beach club?

Can complacent people become numb to injustice?

What has the world become?

What happened to the word of Lord almighty, God?

Love your neighbor as you would yourself and to love God with

all your heart mind and soul.

Have the disgusting antichrists taken over?

I would gladly have my head cut off in the name of Jesus Christ,

Lord Almighty!

"Little children, it is the last hour; and as you have heard that

the Antichrist is coming, even now many antichrists have come,

by which we know that is the last hour." 1 John 2:18

Being powerful and wealthy will present many evils. Lucifer will

abound your soul.

The devil loves to attack children. It can possess the child's mind permanently. This is the vicious cycle for another antichrist in the making.

Many times, Satan will attack children through loved ones.

I was almost there. I was an antichrist at one time. The devil was taking my life little by little. I was destroying everyone in my path. Thank God, Lucifer did not turn me into a murderer or PEDOPHILE!

There are humans not capable of compassion or empathy. This means you could kill or rape someone, and sleep well the same night!

"The Millionaire Beach Club" was already too far gone. Rich and wealthy sociopaths infiltrated the beach with illegal business. The Mafia made sure everything went as planned. Everyone involved gets a piece of the pie. Local people stay alive by keeping quiet.

How can we end crime in order to weed out the evil? First, we must end world hunger and poverty. People have no choice but to work for criminal enterprises to support their families.

Parents will sacrifice their children to feed the family.

It would be amazing if the *righteous* wealthy could help end this

horrible dilemma. Their monthly contributions will provide food

and housing plus education.

Wishful thinking huh?

So, a lot of humanity lives in difficulty. This creates insecurity.

This is how the devil infiltrates the mind. We can beat Satan

because it only controls your mind.

I used to idolize wrath and lust. I was a racist, misogynist and

drug addict. I did not give a shit about anyone but myself! *We*

are seeing this today in America with the careless attitude of

the Covid-19 coronavirus pandemic.

I should be dead or in prison by now.

I am living proof that an antichrist can change after

accepting Jesus.

AUSTIN POLICE DEPARTMENT
Press Release

Name: RIVERA, DAVID
DOB: ▮▮▮▮▮▮▮   Arrest Date: 7/13/2003
Race: HISPANIC
Sex: MALE
Eyes: BROWN
Hair: BLACK
Height: 510
Weight: 225

Are sick and evil antichrists capable of rehabilitation?

Narcissistic sociopaths are only reachable by God. Only Jesus

can save them.

Why do people become pedophiles?

Is it fear of vulnerability during intimacy?

Is it fear of rejection?

Indeed, wealth will give you access to almost anything.

Does a life like this, create evil curiosity?

Are insecure people capable of being monsters once given

power and authority?

Power is intoxicating.

The devil will deceive your mind.

You must have an identity in Jesus.

GOD'S LAW FORBIDS SEX WITH CHILDREN!

According to Wikipedia, a pedophile is someone who has a

sexual interest to a child under the age of 13 years. Currently,

there is no definitive answer as to why one becomes a

pedophile. Wikipedia also states that there is no known cure.

There have been many reports within the clergy. Even, among

the famous.

The wealthy are capable of being evil. Most criminals are

controlled by their lust for money and power.
Quite possibly, a "Millionaire Beach Club," could exist ordinarily

for the right price...

Is America already there?

The country we visited, must have had an anti-extradition law.

Criminals stay if they continue to bring in business. Everyone

involved is compensated. Even the local economies benefit.

This is probably why- we were nearly attacked in the water.

You have seen this happen in many countries.

I believe in my heart- America is the last *"safe"* frontier for all

humanity.

I remember what my beloved Godmother, Martha, told me

about her father, Juan Galindo. He legally immigrated their

family into the United States during the late 1950's.

He told her:

"This is a country where bad people can't use their influence

and money to commit atrocities to the innocent."

I believe our democracy is at risk of becoming a *full blown*

"Millionaire Beach Club": a country controlled by rich selfish

antichrists.

We must never tolerate horrible crime such as child trafficking!

As of today, our judicial system does not allow for anyone to be

above the law. We must protect this because it is really a

privilege.

Now I understand why my travel partner said, "God Bless
America!"

"I pledge allegiance to the flag of the United States of America
and to the republic for which it stands, one nation under God,
indivisible, with liberty and justice for all."

www.ingramcontent.com/pod-product-compliance
Lightning Source LLC
Chambersburg PA
CBHW041225270326
41933CB00006B/215